the

HEART

of the matter

THE GOD-FOCUSED SCHOOL

The Heart of the Matter: The God-Focused School
Written by Frank Hamrick
Layout and Design by Shannon Brown

Published by Positive Action For Christ, Inc.

CONTENTS

INTRODUCTION

For more than 35 years, the staff of Positive Action For Christ has labored to reach the next generation and to give young people a passion for God and a burden for the souls of men. We have often said, "It is youth or consequences." Either we reach youth today, or we will suffer the consequences tomorrow. The future of our nation, the future of the Church, and the future of our world resides in its youth. Dealing with this reality is at the heart of Positive Action's mission.

We have faithfully partnered with local church youth ministries and with Christian schools both to train leadership and to produce curricula and resources that will impact the next generation for God. But what do we mean when we say that we are trying to "reach" today's youth? What is a church youth ministry really trying to accomplish? For what purpose do youth groups, Christian schools, Christian camps, youth publishing houses, and myriads of other youth ministries exist? This book makes the case that the greatest purpose of any youth ministry is to produce a generation of youth with a passion for Christ and a burden for the souls of men. For more on this topic, call to order our free CD, "Encourage A Passion For God."

Youth ministry (and Christian schools are at the forefront of youth ministry) is not about behavior modification, but heart transformation. The Christian school is not about teaching youth how to live, but about magnifying the majesty of God. The Christian school is not primarily about academics, but about attitude. The Christian school is not about sports, but spirituality.

Christian school teachers are not behaviorists, but cardiologists. They are not dispensers of facts, but magnifying glasses ("...Christ shall be magnified in my body, whether it be by life, or by death..." Phil. 1:20). They are not so much teachers as disciplers. They teach, not so that students will have good grades and academic knowledge, but so that their students will have a heart for God and zeal to take God's name to the ends of the earth. They realize that their ministry is a matter of the heart. This is the "heart" of the matter.

Christian ministries must be about God's business exclusively if they are to be Christian ministries, and God's business is single—to glorify His name. Old Testament references abound as to God's single purpose. David reminds Israel that God saved them "for his name's sake," that He might make His power known (Ps. 106:8). Isaiah quotes God as saying "I am the Lord; that is My name: and My glory will I not give to another..." (42:8); and "I will not give My glory to another" (48:11); and "I will gather all nations and tongues; and they shall come, and see My glory" (66:18). Ezekiel quotes God as saying that the only reason He brought Israel back from captivity (and the only reason He is raising her up today) was "for My name's sake" (Ezek. 20:14). So it has ever been, and so it will always be.

God has just one purpose—the exaltation of His name and the magnification of His glory. Therefore, a Christian ministry must have just one purpose if it will be a legitimate Christian ministry—the magnification of His glorious name. His name reveals His character, His power, His works, and His person. The most fundamental question in any form of Christian youth ministry is, "How can we most effectively magnify His name to the next generation?" Our own ministry has considered this question for many years. Over time we identified several essential objectives that our organization could pursue:

1. Help churches develop godly parents because parents are paramount in determining the direction youth take in life.

2. Awaken more churches to the imperative of reaching youth because local churches are vital in accomplishing this goal.

3. Help Christian schools graduate godly youth by providing solid Bible curriculum for them.

Over the years Positive Action has been used in each of these areas. However, in recent years we have realized that there is something even more fundamental to discipling youth. While godly parents, church youth groups, and Christian school Bible curriculum are the key institutions in the process of developing godly youth, they must know how to do it. Therefore, we have made a few subtle changes to our mission. Today our goals are:

1. To help churches develop *God-focused* parents because parents are paramount in determining the direction youth take in life.

2. To awaken more churches to the imperative of *instilling a passion for the exaltation of God's name* in youth because local churches are vital in accomplishing this goal.

3. To help Christian schools graduate youth *who are in awe of their God* by providing solid Bible curriculum for them.

Godly parents are really God-focused parents. Some define "godly parents" as those who go to church, have high standards for their children, and strive to teach them to know and obey the Bible. If this is true godliness, then it falls short of what youth need and what God desires. Children need parents who are dimensionally deeper than the "godliness" described above. They need parents who have an abiding love for the Lord and who know how to magnify His name to their children in such a way that their children do not simply conform to their parents' lifestyle, but they fall in love with their parents' God!

David told his son, "And thou, Solomon my son, know thou the God of thy father, and serve him with a perfect heart and with a willing mind…If thou seek him, he will be found of thee." (1 Chr. 28:9). David was not just godly; he was God-focused! He desired more than mere conformity. He was concerned that Solomon would know his father's God and would serve Him with a "perfect heart and with a willing mind." He wanted Solomon's service to come from the pure motive of love and awe for his father's God.

Neither do church youth groups always produce God-fearing youth. They often produce youth who are "churchy" but worldly; moral but not in awe of God. They produce youth who conform to a Christian lifestyle without a God-loving heart. Christian school graduates often have academic knowledge but little passion for God. While they were students, they may have learned the language and adopted the lifestyle of the church, but they rejected a true heart for God. Why is this true? Are we failing? Are we overlooking a key ingredient of discipleship? Or is it simply a "sign of the times"? Perhaps it is "just the age in which we live," as one teacher said to this author.

I have come to believe that a key ingredient has been overlooked in our ministries. Asaph referred to it in Psalm 78 as a "dark saying of old." By that he meant that there was a truth in his day that was "dark" in the sense that it was overlooked and forgotten. At the same time it was "old" in the sense that it had been clearly taught to his nation some 500 years earlier. The truth is then revealed in the verses that follow. In particular this overlooked and forgotten truth was that youth needed to be taught the praises, strength, and works of God. In essence, Asaph was saying that the forgotten truth was a *focus on God.*

It is paradoxically true that the simplest of truths are both the most important *and* the most overlooked. That accurately describes the phrase "God-focused." While no one would deny that all Christian homes and ministries should be God-focused, little effort is expended to consider whether or not our ministries and homes are truly God-focused. We simply assume they are and spend little time thinking about it.

Christian school teachers are surely God-focused, aren't they? If they teach from a theocentric perspective, they quote Scripture, and they talk about God and Jesus, aren't they God-focused? But *are* we? Are our Christian schools God-focused because they have chapel; because they preach and teach the Bible; or because they talk about the Lord? Or is there more to being God-focused than at first meets the eye? The purpose of this booklet is to focus our thinking on this one fundamental question. Are we God-focused? Don't forget. The heart of the matter is a matter of the heart.

CHAPTER 1

WHAT A GOD-FOCUSED MINISTRY IS NOT

B efore we go further, we need to define what we do not
mean by a God-focused ministry.

NOT ABOUT ACADEMICS

While academics are important in Christian education,
they are not the ultimate purpose of Christian education. Academic success is not equivalent to spiritual maturity. Yet, many
Christian schools seem to stress grades, homework, and academic achievement far more than spiritual growth. They assume that the Church is responsible for spiritual growth, while
the school is responsible for academic growth.

We must never forget that Christian schools are not just
schools. They are *Christian* schools. And if they are distinctly
Christian, then they must necessarily be foremost about spiritual growth, godly knowledge, and instilling God-focused,

God-fearing, and God-loving hearts in their students. Sadly, graduates cross the stage to receive diplomas while teachers recite their academic and extracurricular achievements with little thought for their love for God and desire to serve Him. Long before the Apostle Paul became a Christian, he had achieved the highest standards of academic excellence in the eyes of the Jewish world.

NOT ABOUT EXTRACURRICULAR ACTIVITIES

Sports and other extracurricular activities certainly have a place in Christian schools. They should not have the main focus, however. Many Christian schools tend to build their schedules around sports events. Booster clubs give far more money to the sports program than to the ministry programs, and the sports heroes are sometimes far more popular than the students who have a heart for God. This does not mean that one cannot be an athlete and have a heart for God. A student can do both, but sadly, so much emphasis is placed on athletics that the emphasis on the spiritual is overshadowed. It seems that our schools turn out more basketball players than Bible teachers and preachers.

Why is this? Is it because we are actually sports-focused rather than God-focused? Do we give more time to music and drama than we give to building a passion for God? Count up the hours of practice and rehearsal, the funds raised by booster clubs, the time taken for travel to games or fine arts festivals, and the time spent building extravagant sets. Think of the time we devote to scheduling and developing the extracurricular programs in our schools. Do our chapels, outreach programs, and Bible classes even get *equal* time, much less *more* time? Is it because we see more enthusiasm in our pep rallies than our chapel services? Is it because we give trophies and rewards to sports stars, but nothing to those with a heart for God?

Athletics can offer a convenient target for our criticism, but even fine arts programs can become a distraction to God-focused discipleship in a Christian school. Excellence in music and drama can cultivate pride and divert our attention from devotion to God just as easily as first-class athletics programs can. Just because musical and speaking talents can be used directly in church ministry does not mean that every application of these talents contributes to authentic worship.

NOT ABOUT A
SOUL-WINNING MINISTRY

While soul-winning (a better term would be the New Testament word "witnessing") is honorable, and it is a vital part of any biblical ministry (Acts 1:8; Matt. 28:19–20), it is not synonymous with the phrase "God-focused." Much that passes for "soul-winning" may be prideful, self-serving, or even contrary to biblical teaching. While witnessing is admirable and necessary, it is not the same thing as a God-focus. There can be no God-focus without evangelism, but there *can* be evangelism without a God-focus (Phil. 1:15–18).

Evangelism can either be the product of a man-focus or the product of a God-focus. Man-focused evangelism is:

- Will-driven. It is motivated by a self-proclaimed fleshly determination to witness. It is driven by the will (from the Greek word *thelo*). Therefore, it is *thelocentric*, or will-centered).

- Guilt-driven. It is motivated by a sermon or challenge to evangelism that leaves us feeling guilty, so we have shamed ourselves to start witnessing.
- Job-driven. Our administration or school board requires it, so we agree to do it.
- Duty-driven. We know that it is our responsibility to witness, so we discipline ourselves to do it.
- Pride-driven. We see that people who witness faithfully receive public acclaim, so we witness in order to gain the praise of men.

True evangelism, however, is God-focused. God-focused evangelism is:

- Passion-driven. It is based on a deep love for God that produces evangelism as a natural part of our life. Therefore, it is *theocentric* (God-centered). No self determination is required. It flows naturally from a heart that is on fire with love for God.
- Grace-driven. It is the product of a heart that is thrilled with the grace of God and wants the whole world to know.

When we understand this principle, we will stop urging our students to witness. Rather than preach for a desired behavior, we target their hearts. Rather than pleading with them to evangelize, we will magnify the glory of God, knowing that as they grow in their love and fear of Him, they will grow in their desire to witness.

When evangelism becomes the purpose of a school rather than the natural product of a passion for God, it degenerates into unbiblical attitudes and methods. The faculty and students may be so concerned about "getting students saved" that evangelism becomes a self-centered contest for numbers and throws out the Holy Spirit in favor of methods guaranteed to get results. Those kinds of "results" usually are not permanent. Man-centered evangelism may produce youth who courageously engage in efforts to conquer souls at a special outreach activity but who are carnal in their daily life. Why? I suggest that the focus is wrong. Their focus is on soul-winning, not on God!

Soul-winning does not guarantee that youth will have a God-focus, but the converse *is* true. A God-focus will produce soul-burdened youth. Do you desire to see your students develop a burden for souls? Then instead of preaching to them about soul-winning, magnify His glory and cultivate a passion for God in their hearts. Like Jeremiah of old, they will be unable to keep their mouths shut (Jer. 20:9)!

NOT ABOUT CONTROLLING BEHAVIOR

Sadly, many schools have become agents of behavioral modification. Their focus is merely on what teens should do and what they shouldn't do. Too often we think that if we can get our students to do right and keep them from doing wrong, then they are just fine in their relationship with God. This mindset produces teaching and preaching designed to change behavior. We call it obedience, but we're really talking about behavior.

However, there is a difference between behavior and obedience. Obedience is driven by a love for God and a desire to obey Him, but behavior is driven by guilt, shame, rules, regulations, and a desire to please authorities or to "get them off my back." A God-focus will produce obedience. Anything else will produce behavior. Let's look more carefully at the forces that drive a behavior-focused ministry.

Behavioral ministries focus on guilt.

We have discovered that if we can make youth feel guilty enough, they will cave in and give up bad habits. Therefore, we drive home the fact that certain practices are sin, and that if they practice these sins, they are not right with God. We then challenge them to give it up in order to get right with God. We tell them that if they are the kind of people they should be, they wouldn't be doing that, whatever "that" is.

Now, we certainly should confront sin, and our youth may not be righteous before God. But something is wrong with this approach. Should we not confront sin? Certainly we should. But the problem is that this approach is not God-focused. A God-focused approach to sin is poles apart from a behavior-driven approach to sin.

Behavioral ministries focus on rules.

While we must have rules and regulations, we must take care that rules and regulations do not govern the conduct of our youth, but rather that our youth are motivated by a love for God and a desire to please Him. Often when they disobey our rules, we focus more on insuring that they are consistently punished than we do on addressing real heart issues. We assume their hearts are not right, but we medicate the behavior rather than the heart!

Obviously, rules are necessary, but many of our rules have nothing to do with spirituality. They may have legitimate purposes: orderliness, efficiency, health, safety, protection of property, creating a better learning environment, respecting authority, and so on. But even legitimate rules, though necessary, do not by themselves produce God-loving youth. Other rules are based on preference, and all too often these are clouded with

Scripture verses that are taken out of context, harsh warnings against breaking these rules, and claims that those who do not follow these rules are not spiritual.

These rules may well produce a wrong view of God. Students mistakenly conclude that God's favor is based on behavior. As long as they follow the rules, everything will be just fine. They fail to see that God wants them to love Him, not simply follow a list of rules created by people. God speaks to this problem in Isaiah 29:13. "Wherefore the Lord said, Forasmuch as this people draw near Me with their mouth, and with their lips do honor Me, but have removed their heart far from Me, and their fear toward Me is taught by the precept of men." Israel's "spirituality" consisted of following rules and traditions laid down by men. They said the right thing, and they followed the rules of men, but their *hearts* were far from God. The same can be true of youth today.

These rules may also produce a wrong view of spirituality. Youth mistakenly assume that the Christian life consists of a list of do's and don'ts. While God is certainly concerned about godly living, sanctification and holiness are far more important than living by rules. At its heart, holiness begins in the heart. It flourishes in a heart that is being conformed to the image of Christ from the inside, not from the outside.

Behavioral ministries are driven by a desire for acceptance.

One of a teen's strongest desires is to be accepted. His behavior is often driven by pressure from other teenagers—peer pressure. It could be pressure from the family. It could be pressure from the church. It could be pressure from the youth group. It could be pressure from the school. Some youth may live in an environment that constantly molds or conforms them to act in a certain way. Soon they learn that life is much easier and hassle-free if they simply conform their lives to behave in a certain fashion. So, we must insure that our efforts to help teens live godly are God-focused and appeal to their love for Him rather than our demands that they behave. Their love for Him will cultivate lasting obedience.

NOT ABOUT BUILDING CHARACTER

Certainly, character building is important, but character, like behavior, can be motivated by many unbiblical forces. A leading youth ministry magazine recently discussed character building as the "end all be all" of youth work. While character is vital, it must not be the focus of our teaching.

True character is not learned; it is produced. It springs out of a mind that is so focused on the Lord that one changes into His image. Ephesians 4:13 tells us that as we "come in…the knowledge of the Son of God" that we will be "a perfect [mature, complete] man." It is knowledge of and meditation on Him that produces character.

Surely, there is nothing wrong with academics, athletics, witnessing, good conduct, rules, regulations, and character development. All of these can be beneficial and even necessary. However, they become detrimental when they are elevated to the central focus of a ministry or when they are mistakenly substituted for godliness. They are good areas of emphasis, but they are not equivalent to a God-focus. If we are not careful, we will substitute these good things for the most vital thing. We will have a good focus, but not a God-focus. The results will be mechanical and temporary rather than spiritual and permanent.

CHAPTER 2

WHAT A GOD-FOCUS IS

Now that we know what a God-focus is *not*, consider what it *is*. Simply put, a God-focused ministry is one in which both the goal and the methods of ministry are designed to magnify the majesty of God so much that young people develop a passion for Him that governs every aspect of their lives. Probably most who read this booklet will have wholehearted agreement with this goal. Is there a Christian teacher, pastor, youth worker, or Sunday school teacher who would not say, "I want youth to have a passion for God that governs every aspect of their lives"?

It is one thing to affirm this goal, but quite another actually to achieve it. Therein lies the million dollar question—how do we give students this life-changing, obedience-governing love for Him? To answer this question, we must examine everything we do as teachers and school administrators. We must scrutinize our methods to insure that they are designed to magnify the majesty of God to such a degree that young people have a passion for God that governs every single aspect of their lives.

For sixteen years I served as youth pastor in Rocky Mount, North Carolina, and I have been the father of four children for many more years than that. During that time, my goal has been that my own children and the teens in my youth group would be constrained by a love for their Lord, their Savior, rather than being driven by my rules and my preaching about certain things, even though those things were important. I realized that I would not always be with them. Their moms and dads would not always be with them. The school would not always be there. But if their hearts were in awe of God and in love with the Lord, that would "keep them" throughout their lives. David's son wisely said, "Keep thy heart with all diligence, for out of it are the issues of life" (Prov. 4:23). Many other Scripture passages likewise support the value of a God-focus. We will consider three in greater detail.

MOSAIC PRINCIPLES FOR GOD-FOCUSED MINISTRY

DEUTERONOMY 8:10–11

[10]When thou hast eaten and art full, then thou shalt bless the LORD thy God for the good land which he hath given thee. [11]Beware that thou forget not the LORD thy God, in not keeping his commandments, and his judgments, and his statutes, which I command thee this day.

Moses warned the children of Israel about their future conquest of Canaan. They would inherit a land of fertile fields and hills filled with iron ore; a land of plentiful water and rain; a climate to support myriads of crops; and a luscious land full of milk and honey. Then He warned them in verse 10 that when they had eaten and were fully satisfied, they must be careful to "bless the Lord…for the good land" that He had given them, and to beware of a dangerous sin—the sin of forgetfulness. "Beware that thou forget not the Lord thy God," he reminds them. Materialism causes one to forget God.

The teacher's imperative is to remind youth constantly of the glories, the grace, and the gifts of God. It is our task to shift their focus from material things to God's majesty.

DEUTERONOMY 6:4–9

4Hear, O Israel: The LORD our God is one LORD: 5And thou shalt love the LORD thy God with all thine heart, and with all thy soul, and with all thy might. 6And these words, which I command thee this day, shall be in thine heart: 7And thou shalt teach them diligently unto thy children, and shalt talk of them when thou sittest in thine house, and when thou walkest by the way, and when thou liest down, and when thou risest up. 8And thou shalt bind them for a sign upon thine hand, and they shall be as frontlets between thine eyes. 9And thou shalt write them upon the posts of thy house, and on thy gates.

Moses had been on the mountain of God for forty days and had been given the law that would guide the nation of Israel for the next 1,500 years. The elders gathered to hear Moses' words and to learn what God had told them to do. To this day, this passage is revered by all religious Jews. They zealously call it the *shema* after the first word used in this passage of Scripture. Taking verse 7 literally, they write the entire passage on a small piece of paper, roll it up, and place it in a box. Then they tie this box to their hand, tie it to their head, or nail it to their doorposts. This passage is like the national anthem of religious Israel. Everything religious Israel did was based on this passage.

Notice how this passage begins. "Hear, O Israel, the Lord our God is one Lord." It begins with a theological statement—with a focus on God. The implication is that the foundation for all that follows in the law is based on a God-focus.

Scholars marvel at the theological implications of verse 4. When we study the grammar and consider the plural and singular references to God, we will see both the great doctrine of monotheism *and* the doctrine of the tri-unity of God. We see in this passage the foundational truths that govern all of Judaism. This great theological statement thereby becomes the foundation for all of Judaism.

This passage is not just about Judaism, however. The *shema* is nothing less than God's design for youth ministry! The passage opens with a revelation of the God of the Bible as the only God of the universe. It continues by outlining the Mosaic principles for youth ministry. So, God's design for youth ministry is founded on *theology*. Yet, there seems to be little theological emphasis today in discipling youth, whether in the church or the school.

Moses continues in verse 4: "And thou shalt love the Lord thy God with all thine heart and with all thy soul and with all thy might. And these words which I command thee this day [the things I'm getting ready to say in this Jewish *shema*] shall be in thine heart and…thou shalt teach them diligently unto thy children" (vs. 7). That is the biblical standard for youth ministry. God gives us the blueprint for reaching the next generation, and it begins with this statement: "The Lord our God is one Lord." It begins with theology.

Moses now addresses the parents, and in doing so he is most concerned with their heart. They should love the Lord their God with all their heart, with all their might, and with all their soul. That is, they must have a passion for Him that pervades every cell and fiber of their bodies. Furthermore, verse 5 tells us that these truths must be in their hearts (not just their heads). What truths is He talking about that must be in their hearts? He is first referring to the truth about God, then to the truth about the rest of His Word.

Has it ever occurred to us that parents must be theologians? So should Christian school teachers because they are also discipling youth. Whether we teach math, science, language arts, sports, music, or history; above all else we must be theologians because our primary responsibility is to bring students face to face with the God of the Bible.

Moses is not finished yet. In the verses that follow he reminds them that once they understand the theology, and once they get beyond their understanding of theology to a genuine love for the God of that theology, then, "Thou shalt teach them to thy children." So where does Christian education begin? Christian education begins with theology. It begins with a God-focus. Moses concludes this portion of Scripture with these words from Deuteronomy 6:10–13:

> [10]*And it shall be when the Lord thy God shall have brought thee into the land which he sware to thy fathers Abraham, Isaac, and Jacob and give thee great and goodly cities, which thou buildest not,*

> *[11] And houses full of goods which thou filledst not, and wells digged, which thou diggedst not, vineyards and olive trees, which thou plantedst not; when thou shalt have eaten and be full; [12] Beware lest you forget the Lord, which brought you out of the land of Egypt, from the house of bondage. [13] Thou shalt fear the Lord thy God, and serve him...*

It is always this way. True service comes from a deep and abiding fear (awe and respect) for Almighty God.

We must not forget that there is a danger to be avoided. The danger Israel faced in 1400 B.C. is the same danger youth face today: materialism. The problem with materialism is that it gets our focus off of God. Just as Israel would live in houses they didn't build and would enjoy food they didn't work for or buy, so today's youth enjoy all the luxuries and benefits of the 21st century without the struggle to pay for it or grow it. They wear clothes that were given to them. They think of TV, video games, iPods, DVDs, cell phones, and computers as necessities, not luxuries. Students are often given an education that cost their parents dearly, but costs the students nothing.

One of the great dangers of our society is that there is simply too much to love. We leave little room for God. Youth can love sports but not love God. They can enjoy their school but not love God. They can relish Spanish, math, or some other academic discipline, but not love God. As a writer, I've learned to use and to love technology. Give me a gift certificate to a technology store, and that is the closest thing to heaven this side of heaven for me! But that same technology that can help me write about Him can also take my heart away from Him. I must be careful. Beware, teacher. Materialism causes us to forget God, and forgetting Him is the most grievous of sins. This is why Moses warns Israel lest they lose their focus on God.

DAVIDIC PRINCIPLES FOR GOD-FOCUSED MINISTRY

PSALM 78

As Deuteronomy 6 gives us the Mosaic principles of youth ministry, so Psalm 78 gives us the Asaphian (or Davidic) principles of youth ministry. The passage was written by Asaph, a disciple of David, and the truths he teaches here about youth work were undoubtedly learned from David, who appointed him as his head musician after several years of working with him.

In verse 4 Asaph, speaking of the things that "our fathers have taught us," says, "we will not hide them from their children shewing to the generation to come the praises of the Lord, and his strength, and his wonderful works that he hath done."

What must we show the generation to come? We must show (teach) them "the praises of the Lord, and his strength, and the wonderful works that he hath done." Thus, Asaph identifies the core curriculum for youth ministry, whether at home, in a church, or in a school. It consists of three major topics: 1) the praises of the Lord, 2) the strength of the Lord, and 3) the works of the Lord. Next, Asaph tells us that the benefit of such a curriculum is "that the generation to come might know them, even the children which should be born; who should arise and declare them to their children, that they might set their hope in God" (vs. 6–7).

Teaching the core curriculum will give youth a theological mindset and thereby cause them to trust God rather than in all the technology, electronic gadgetry, houses, bank accounts, and cars that we possess. They will rely on God rather than putting all their trust in their youth pastor, their parents, their church, or their school.

CHAPTER 3

THE FOURFOLD EMPHASIS OF A GOD-FOCUS

THEOLOGY PROPER, NOT JUST BIBLE

We should not minimize the Bible. True theology comes from the Bible, but much theology today is derived from personal experience rather than the Word. So, if we are to understand theology, we *must* look to the Word as our reliable, authoritative source. However, we can study the Bible and miss God! We can look for theology and miss theology proper. We can study all kinds of doctrine and miss the very center of all theology—the knowledge of God.

The Pharisees were guilty of this sin. In John 5:39 the Lord rebukes them for their detailed study of the Old Testament accompanied by their failure to see the God of the Old Testament. I often tell students, "Don't study the Word of God!" When they look at me in surprise, I then say, "Instead, study the God of the Word." This book is about Him, not about facts, stories, and history. Neither is the Bible written simply to be a manual for living. The Bible is a revelation of God. The first book of the Bible begins with the words, "In the beginning God," and the last book begins with "The revelation of Jesus Christ." From beginning to end, this book was written to reveal the glory and majesty of the Godhead.

It is all too easy to teach the Bible as an academic book or as a book on behavior and miss the whole point of the Bible. Notice Asaph's instruction in Psalm 78:4: "We will not hide them from their children, shewing to the generation to come the praises of the Lord, his strength and the wonderful works he hath done." Asaph didn't see the Bible as a manual for living! He saw it as a revelation of the Godhead.

John Calvin said, "There is no knowing that does not begin with knowing God." God is the foundational truth. Moses proclaims it in Deuteronomy 6, and Asaph agrees in Psalm 78. Scores of other verses in the Bible attest to the same truth. But sadly, theology proper is one of the most neglected truths in our schools. I fear that we talk about everything *but* Him. If the Christian school is about Christian education, then the most important and foundational subject of all must be theology proper.

Sadly, we often teach the Bible without being God-focused. We can tell the stories of David, Moses, or Esther, but fail to see God in those passages. Yet, those stories were not written to reveal how great people were, but how great God was! When students hear the story of Moses, do they leave your class in awe of Moses or in awe of Moses' God?

Scripture is itself God-focused. It is God's self-revelation. It is not a book of moralistic teaching. Students are not to imitate

David. They must be conformed to the image of Christ, and the only way that happens is by focusing their gaze on Christ in His Word and exercising themselves to be like Him. As students see God in Scripture, the Holy Spirit transforms them from the inside out into the "same image" they are beholding (1 Cor. 3:18). Beholding David will inspire. Beholding David's *God* will transform.

As you teach a passage of Scripture, you should ask God-focused questions such as: 1) What does God do in this passage? 2) What does God reveal about Himself (His attributes and character)? 3) What does this passage teach about how God works in our lives? Such questions are designed to get the focus off of Abraham, Joseph, or Daniel, and onto the one Scripture was written to reveal.

THE CORE CURRICULUM

If we return our attention to the words of Asaph in Psalm 78, we will receive direction from God about three core elements of the curriculum that we need to be teaching to our children.

The praises of the Lord

What are the praises of the Lord? The praises of the Lord refer to God's attributes, His character, His nature, and His essence. They describe all that He is. Asaph tells us that youth need to be focused on the attributes and character of God.

The strength of the Lord

His strength may refer to the names of God. Proverbs 18:10 declares, "The name of the Lord is a strong tower: the righteous runneth into it and is safe." What does it mean to run to the name of God? How does one run to the name of God? Do young people use the names of God to give them faith, strength, courage, and victory to overcome worry, doubt, fear, and compromise? (Do Christian teachers run to God's names?) Do youth use the names of God as a source of strength in times of danger? Do they use His names for courage? Do they or we even *know* His names and what they mean? Do we know the meaning of *El-Shaddai*, and do we call upon *El-Shaddai* at the appropriate time? Do our students know when to run to the name *El-Shaddai*?

What about *Yahweh-Nissi*? How often do your students remember that name, or how often do you talk of God as *Yahweh-Nissi* to your students? Asaph and other Old Testament writers use many different names for God, depending on the situation. Perhaps our failure to understand and practice this principle signals a general lack of the knowledge of God. The God-focused teacher will teach students the names of God and how to seek refuge in His names.

The works of God

Finally, Asaph mentions the wonderful works of God. We often admonish people to study the Word of God, but how often do we challenge them to study the works of God? The Bible mentions the works of God hundreds of times and commands us to declare His works, not just His Word, to mankind.

What are the works of God? Do we enumerate them? Do we catalog them? Do we write them in a book? Do we declare them to others? Do we thank God for them? Do we study them? The Bible asks us to do each of these. Look up the word "works" and study how it is used in the Bible. You will be enriched.

Future faith is based on the knowledge of past providence. If we would produce a generation that puts its confidence in God, then we must diligently teach them His works. When David faced Goliath, his faith was driven, in part, by his memory of two past works of God in his life—when God delivered him from the mouth of a lion and from the paw of a bear. The same God that gave him those victories would now give him victory over "this uncircumcised Philistine." His understanding of the works of God in the past gave him faith for the future.

We challenge youth to godly behavior, but we fail to give them the heart for it. For example, we might say, "We need more youth who will stand like David and not bow down to the giants of this world. We need youth who are not afraid to stand against the world!" This may draw a chorus of "amens" from other adults, but it all too often only frustrates youth. They know how we want them to behave, but they haven't the slightest idea how or why they should do it.

We cry out for David's behavior, but we fail to give them David's secret. David didn't stand against Goliath because his teacher had challenged him to "be like Samuel," or to "stand like Joshua." David stood his ground because of his strong faith in God's past works and because of his fierce love for a God who had been mocked. We want youth to behave like David, but we fail to show them David's heart.

Consider one question. Why was David, "David"? Where did he get such faith and courage? It wasn't because Samuel had challenged him to be like Joshua. David didn't repent of his cowardice at a "Samuel Campaign." He didn't go forward, get down on his knees, and confess, "Lord, by Thy grace I'm going to be like Joshua the rest of my life." No. David became a champion for God because of his knowledge of God. Read the

Psalms, and you will quickly see that David was in love with his God. "My heart is fixed," he declared. His heart was fixed on his God.

David's Psalms are filled with references to the works of God. His writings give evidence of much meditation on God's providence. He says that the stars, the sun, the trees, storms, lightning, clouds, rain, victories in battles, victories over a bear and a lion, and other such works of God are all his delight. This knowledge controlled David's conduct.

When we say, "Be like David," are we not actually challenging youth to change their behavior? Are we not confessing that we're more concerned with their behavior than with their hearts? This is moralistic teaching, but it is not theological teaching. Give your students David's heart, and you will not have to tell them to stand against the giants. The desire and courage to do so will rise up within them.

If David had simply been trying to follow the example of Joshua, he might have hesitated. He might have thought, "I can't remember what Joshua did. Oops, Joshua never faced a giant like Goliath! Now what?"

The Christian life is not about imitating another person. It is not about following moralistic teaching. It is not even about having character. It is not about following a set of rules. Rather, it is about reacting to a right knowledge of God. Youth will be like David when they learn to focus on David's God. If we want a generation of youth to be like David, we must help them to love the same God that David loved. We must help them to have the same intimacy with God that David possessed. Once youth have that intimacy, that understanding, and that passion for God, we will not have to tell them to be like David.

HEART OVER CONFORMITY

A God-focused school will emphasize heart over conformity. David puts it this way in Psalm 51:6: "Thou desirest truth in the inward parts and in the hidden part Thou wilt make me to know wisdom. The sacrifices of God are a broken spirit. A broken and contrite heart, O God, Thou will not despise."

Once more David and Moses agree. In Deuteronomy 6 Moses had said, "These things that I command you this day must be in thy heart…and thou shalt teach them diligently unto thy children."

Does this mean that God is not concerned with outward conduct? Of course not. For example, Moses warns the people to "Beware that thou forget not the Lord thy God in not keeping his commandments" (Deut. 8:11). Here the emphasis is on conduct. We must always remember the relationship between "being" and "doing." *Being* has to do with who I am; it has to do with my heart. *Doing* has to do with how I behave. Both are important, but *being* cannot be faked, and it cannot be forced. *Doing*, on the other hand, can be sourced in scores of motives, some of which are righteous and some of which are very sinful and selfish. God wants obedience from a pure heart, rather than behavior that is either learned, forced, or motivated by selfishness.

If we are not careful, our schools will produce youth who say the right things and do the right things, but for all the wrong reasons. A pastor once boasted to this author that you wouldn't see a short skirt on any girl or long hair on any guy in his school because he preached about these standards in every chapel. Yet, his youth pastor confessed that the youth group was as ungodly as they could be. What was the problem? They had outwardly conformed to a wrong emphasis from the leadership.

When we emphasize academics, or conformity to rules, or behavior over the spiritual condition of the heart, we produce New Testament Pharisees. They knew every detail of the Old Testament, they were sticklers for rules, they counted and cataloged the commandments, and they grievously policed behavior, but they had little heart for God. They were fooled by their own zeal! They assumed that their assiduous study of the Torah and their fastidious practice of every detail of the law was proof of their righteousness. They would boast that they were the most zealous of any sect for their God. They confused zeal for the law with righteousness. Christ denounced their zeal and reminded them that the Old Testament was a revelation of Him. In their zeal for the keeping, they overlooked the Christ.

To reach the heart of youth, we must do more than preach to them or teach academic facts. If we would reach their hearts, we must disciple them. A study of New Testament discipleship can be summed up simply as "spending time with Christ." That's how the disciples were discipled. They simply spent time with Him. If youth are to be discipled today, then 1) we must spend time with them out of class, and 2) they must spend time with Christ.

Teachers must demonstrate a genuine love for Almighty God, a longing for Him, a thirst for Him, and a passion for Him that their students sense merely by being around their teacher. Before they begin to love God, they must see their mentors loving Him. As they spend time with you, they should be able to see how truth and theology proper are fleshed out in your life and how they can be demonstrated in their own lives. The disciples were disciples because they spent time with Christ, followed Christ, and learned from Christ.

In Isaiah 1:11–15 God accuses Israel of having right behavior but a sinful heart. Paraphrasing the passage, God says, "You're praying and sacrificing, and I'm sick of it because it's not coming from your heart." Their conduct was nothing more than outward conformity. Yet, David had declared, "Behold, thou desirest truth in the inward parts: and in the hidden part thou shalt make me to know wisdom" (Ps. 51:6).

Christian schools must pursue obedience rather than behavior. We must recognize that only a deep love for God will produce obedience. As a parent I had to be careful that I was not driving and forcing my children to behave a certain way because they were my children. Instead, I wanted them to obey because they loved the Lord with all their heart, with all their mind, and with all their might. This was sometimes difficult to do because controlling external behavior is much easier than producing love-based obedience.

We are talking about a mindset for teachers and administrators. Too often we have become behaviorists when in reality we need to be cardiologists. Cardiology comes from two words, "heart" (*kardia*) and "word" (*logos*). Isn't that what we should combine in our schools—the heart and the Word? We must so magnify the majesty of Christ that our students will have transformed hearts! *We must become experts at instilling an awe of God in the hearts of youth.* This is the heart of the matter.

THE INNER MAN
OVER PERFORMANCE

The God-focused school will emphasize the inner man over performance. Once more, Psalm 78 speaks to this. The children of Ephraim were armed with bows and were taught how to fight. They could hit a target at 100 feet with ease. They were experts at warfare. However, they were no good in battle because they were cowards on the inside.

The temptation to be more interested in training youth to perform than with building and shaping the inner man is subtly enticing. It can be far too easy for Christian schools to combine a worldly philosophy of performance and competition with an award system designed to honor the best performers. The emphasis on competition in music, speech, and athletic competition can be both helpful and dangerous. While it can be valuable for youth to develop their skills in music and speech, these activities can quickly degenerate into a competitive performance rather than a tool for ministry.

Schools can successfully manage such competition with the right attitude. They can encourage students to understand that these skills can help them serve the God they love and that they are not merely an opportunity to beat another school. An athletics program can be used to provide opportunities for discipleship and to teach lessons of self-discipline and self-denial—lessons that translate directly to the daily walk of a believer.

For years ProTeens, the youth ministry division of Positive Action For Christ, faced this problem with the scoring system and competition that it sponsored. Some youth performed spiritual disciplines for points or to get rewards at the end of the year. If the youth leader was not careful, he would emphasize point scoring over internal transformation of the heart. Performance in itself is not bad, but when the performance and the reward become more important than building the inner man, it is counter-productive.

SPIRITUAL DISCIPLINES OVER SPORTS

Finally, Christian schools must emphasize spiritual disciplines over physical activity. We know that exercise profits a little, but godliness is profitable for all things. A God-focused school will emphasize those disciplines that lead to godliness, not merely physical prowess. We will discuss five of them below.

MEDITATION ON GOD IN THE WORD

Today's youth need to learn the art of biblical meditation. In fact, Christian teachers need to learn this art as well. We must differentiate between right and wrong kinds of meditation. Pop culture utilizes meditation. Medical rehab centers emphasize meditation. Psychologists and advocates of the paranormal talk about transcendental meditation. These forms of meditation are primarily centered on the individual. Teachers of meditation encourage their subjects to relax by closing their eyes and consciously imagining themselves on a desert island or in their favorite place. They teach them to relax their bodies from their toes up by first thinking about their toes and consciously "feeling" them relax. Then they think about their ankles and try to relax them as they "feel" how they feel. Eventually, they progress through their whole bodies. Others lead their subjects to "self-realization" through meditation. The problem with these types of meditation is that the subjects meditate on the wrong thing—themselves.

Biblical meditation, however, is focused on God. When one meditates biblically, he ponders the wonders and works of the Almighty. Beware lest you meditate on the Bible and not on God. To put it accurately, we should meditate *in* the Bible, but not *on* the Bible! Stated another way, we must meditate *on* God *in* the Bible. He is to be our focus. Such meditation on God in His Word will transform our lives.

SCRIPTURE MEMORY

Lovers of God will be lovers of His Word, and Scripture memory will be an automatic response. Still, we should not memorize verses simply for the sake of memorizing verses. There should be a strategic plan to know God better through Scripture memory. While we encourage students to memorize whole passages of Scripture, we need to encourage them to memorize verses based on Asaph's core curriculum—the attributes of God, the names of God, and the works of God.

PRAYER

Perhaps the greatest evidence that we are God-focused is our prayer life. The more I think about Him, the more I find myself talking to Him. The more I'm distracted by other things, the less I pray. A God-focus will lead to a prayer-focus. They go hand-in-hand. Think about Him, and you will soon find yourself talking to Him. Recently I've been thinking about God as my "best friend"—as one who is always with me, sitting beside me in the car or with me in my study. That thought has led me simply to talk to Him—about everything—just like I would if my best earthly friend were sitting there. I actually find myself laughing with Him and sometimes even complaining to Him and questioning Him about things I don't understand. Think of Him often, and you will talk to Him often.

Prayer should be a primary part of our classroom instruction, not something we do just at the beginning of the class. Sadly, those prayers at the beginning of a class are often too hastily uttered and too perfunctory. We give the impression that we are simply going through the motions of praying. We quickly get it said and get it behind us so we can get to the more important matter of covering the material in our textbook.

WITNESSING

Two forces lead students and teachers to witness: external behavioral forces and a love for God. If we are in awe of God, we have to proclaim it. God-focused witnessing is not done because we're required to, because we get points for it, or because it's a nice group activity. It's not done because I might look like some weirdo if I don't. It's not done because the school board or administrator requires it of me. No, those are all forms of "behavioral" witnessing. God-focused witnessing is done because I love Him and I simply have to tell people about my glorious Lord.

Schools must be careful that they do not shame students into witnessing. Rather, they must talk so much of the glories, the grace, and the gospel of God that the students find themselves sharing their excitement about Him with others in a very natural way.

DAILY STUDY IN GOD'S WORD

Every teacher in a God-focused school will have devotions with his or her students. It may be no more than a single verse with a few brief sentences of explanation and a prayer. An elementary teacher may have the luxury of going longer, but when we are excited about the Lord, we will share it with our class.

Of course, the "devotion" may not be at a set time. It may come in the middle of a history lesson or in the middle of conjugating verbs. It may be something a student says that triggers it. Devotions may simply be a small parenthesis during the day when a God-focused teacher finds himself quite naturally talking about the works, the Word, or the wonders of God. It is a sad day when we talk more about sports or the weather than of God. What is the emphasis of your class and of your school? Is it on academic instruction or other school-related matters, or is it on the majesty of the Lord?

CHAPTER 4

THE EFFECTS OF A GOD-FOCUS

ON HOW WE VIEW AND CONFRONT SIN

Why is it important that we have a God-focus? One reason is because it will affect the way we handle sin. How do you deal with sin in your class? Do you deal with it so that students learn how their sin violates the character of God? If not, a God-focus will fundamentally change the way you handle problems in your classroom.

Years ago, I was preparing my youth group to attend The Wilds summer camp in North Carolina. In those days we had volleyball and basketball competitions between the ProTeen clubs that attended. Our teens were practicing volleyball the week before camp when some of them got extremely angry, throwing the ball and yelling at each other. I immediately jumped into the explosion and tried to calm everyone down. I told them to sit on the volleyball court, and I began to berate them for their conduct. I told them that if this was their attitude, we would not field a team at The Wilds. They dropped their heads and listened, and soon one of them said, "Frank, we're sorry. We wouldn't hurt you for anything in the world. We promise we will not embarrass you at The Wilds."

I was stunned. I realized that they were focused on me! My response was something like this: "What did you just say? This has nothing to do with me. We're not talking about me. This is about your Lord. Do you realize what you just did to your God?"

I then launched into a focus on Him. I described the love Christ had for them—a love that brought Him to earth to die for the very sin they had just committed. I then described the kind of sacrifice that Christ made for us on the cross. I spoke of the nails piercing His wrists and the spear in His side. I then concluded by saying, "Look into those eyes. Those eyes were looking at you. They were looking at this very moment. They saw you with that bad temper, and Jesus was thinking, 'I'm dying for what you will one day do on a volleyball court. I'm suffering on this cross to pay for that awful sin in your heart.'"

Some of the teens started to weep, and soon they asked to pray. "Lord, we wouldn't do anything to hurt you," they said. "Lord, you've done too much for us. We're sorry we broke your heart." In that moment I learned the difference in a "guilt-focused" approach to sin and a "God-focused" approach.

Romans 3:23 defines sin. It is falling short of His glory. His glory is His attributes. All sin is a violation of the character of God. Every sin is a violation of one or more of His attributes. If your students do not know the attributes of God, they do not know what sin is. Why is lying wrong? Lying is wrong because God is truth. Lying violates the character of God. It is our responsibility to teach them both the attributes of God and the sins associated with breaking that attribute. When we trace all sin back to an attribute of God, our students will look at sin differently. They will pray as David prayed: "Against thee, thee only, have I sinned."

ON HOW WE VIEW SALVATION

A God-focus will change your approach to salvation. Much of modern evangelism is man-centered. Salvation is often presented as though God sits helplessly in heaven hoping that someone will believe in Him before it's too late. This is contrary to the God presented in the Bible. The Bible teaches that God is in total control of salvation. Jonah looked back on his deliverance from the belly of the whale and exulted, "Salvation is of the Lord" (Jonah 2:9). Earlier, he had declared, "Thou brought up my life from corruption, O LORD my God" (2:6). Jonah realized his helpless condition and that his salvation was totally from the Lord.

Paul said it this way in 2 Corinthians 2:14: "Now thanks be unto God, which always causeth us to triumph in Christ, and maketh manifest the savor of his knowledge by us in every place." The phrase "causeth us to triumph in Christ" would be better translated, "who leads us in his triumph in Christ." It is a graphic portrayal of a conqueror returning to Rome with the spoils of his conquest. He makes a grand entrance into the city followed by a long parade of conquered people and possessions. Paul borrows this imagery in describing Christ as leading us in His victory parade. We are His conquered possession.

Paul again uses such imagery in Colossians 2:15: "And having spoiled principalities and powers, he made a show of them openly, triumphing over them in it" (their defeat by the cross of Christ). The "principalities and powers" may refer to actual rulers of the day, or more likely, to spiritual authorities—Satan and his demonic hosts. Christ "spoiled" them at the cross. That is, He disarmed them and ransomed us from their grasp. Once again, Paul makes reference to Christ's conquest in Ephesians 4:8 when he speaks of Christ leading captive a host of captives at His resurrection. So, Scripture teaches that salvation is a conquest by God. I do not obtain my salvation. Rather, God conquers my soul by triumphing over death, hell, and the grave at the Cross and in His Resurrection.

One reason so many doubt their salvation is because of a man-focused approach to salvation and to the gospel. The following dialogue is typical of a modern gospel presentation:

> *"Are you saved?"*
> *"Yes."*
> *"How do you know it? What did you do?"*

There is a problem with this line of questioning The focus is on man and not on God. The focus is on what the believer did rather than on what God did. Over the years I sought to change the way I asked people if they were saved. It has been difficult to do because I had developed a habit of asking what the believer did for salvation. Now I question a person about salvation this way:

"Has God ever saved your soul?" If the answer is yes, I reply, "How do you know?" If the person says that he knows because he believed, I then ask, "But, did God save you when you believed?" They may answer, "Of course He did. The Bible says that if I believe, He will save me." I reply, "That is not necessarily so. The devils believe and they aren't saved. The question is not what you have done; the question is what God has done. Did God save your soul? What has God done?" "Well, I went forward at an invitation," he may reply. "No, I'm not asking what you did. What has God done? Prove your own salvation to me. Prove to me that God conquered your soul and saved you when you believed."

That is a totally different approach to salvation and a different question entirely. So, what is significant about asking, "Has God ever saved you?" rather than asking, "Are you saved?" The significance is in the focus of the question. The salvation question should not be focused on what man did for salvation, but on what God has done. Because of our man-centered approach, many people still doubt their salvation because they worry that they didn't "really believe," or that they didn't have enough faith, or that they didn't fully understand what was going on at the time. In each case, they are focusing on what they did.

However, when one focuses on what God did, he will approach the subject of his salvation differently. When I ask one to prove to me that God saved him, what I am asking is for him to show me the evidence of a divine work of grace in his heart. In other words, I want to know if he has a hunger to know the Word; if he has a desire to grow in the Lord and to please Him; if he has a desire to be around other Christians; and if he has seen changes in his attitude toward sin, the Bible, church attendance, and worldly amusements.

Second Corinthians 5:17 tells us that if God has saved a person, she will be a new creature, that old things will start passing away, and that all things will become new. In other words, there will be supernatural changes taking place in her mind and attitude toward righteousness and unrighteousness. I look for those evidences rather than a simple answer that she knows she is saved because she "believed." I am looking for what God, the almighty Conqueror and Transformer of people's hearts has done, rather than what she may have attempted to do. We must remember that there is a belief that does not save. There is a simple mental assent to facts, but that is not saving faith. The emphasis of the salvation issue must not be centered on whether or not teens have "believed," but on whether or not God has done a work of grace in their hearts.

ON HOW WE VIEW HOLINESS

When one has a God-focus, it will change the way he approaches personal holiness. Sadly, we look at holiness as little more than turning from sin. However, 1 Thessalonians defines holiness differently. Holiness is turning to God from idols (1 Thess. 1:9). Teens may separate from all manner of sin, but still not be "holy" because holiness is separation *to* someone, not simply separation *from* something. Teens may turn from idols and still not turn to God. But they can never turn *to* God without turning *from* idols!

Some are quick to emphasize what youth should turn *from*, but seldom talk about what they need to turn *to*. Yet, if we can get youth to turn to God, to "look full in His wonderful face," then "the things of earth will grow strangely dim in the light of His glory and grace." When you are overcome with His glory and grace, your idols will begin to fall away. Here again we see that a God-focus is a mindset. When we understand it, we will change our approach to many aspects of the Christian life.

ON HOW WE VIEW SANCTIFICATION

The God-focused mindset will also change the way we approach sanctification, or spiritual growth. It seems that the doctrine of progressive sanctification is presented far too often in terms of human effort. To overcome anger, we might follow a "five-step" program. We reduce the Christian life to a list of sins and steps for overcoming them. We make much of the commands in Ephesians 4, but we forget that chapter 4 is based on a "therefore" (4:1). The implication is that all that Paul commands us to do in chapter 4 is based on all that comes before in chapters 1–3. If we do not understand the basis of chapter 4, our efforts at sanctification will be based on ourselves, not the power of God.

Paul speaks of walking worthy of our calling in Ephesians 4:1. He then defines the worthy walk in the verses that follow. We are to walk with lowliness of meekness, with longsuffering, and with forbearance. However, these qualities are the product of realizing the great truths of chapters 1–3—truths that focus on the person of God and His plan for mankind. Chapter 4 then reminds us that we are to be perfected through "the knowledge of the Son of God" (vs. 13); that we are to grow up "into Him" (vs. 15); and that we are to be "renewed in the spirit of your mind" (vs. 23). This last phrase has reference to the transforming work of meditating on God in the Word as shown in Romans 12:1–2 and 1 Corinthians 3:18.

Romans 12:1–2 parallels Ephesians 4:23 by imploring us to be transformed by "renewing" our minds. Second Corinthians 3:18 tells us how to do that—through meditation on the glory of God (His attributes) in the mirror of God's Word. As we continually look for His majesty, His attributes, His works, His glory, and His grace in the Word, we are gradually transformed (the same word found in Romans 12:2) into His very image.

We can conclude that sanctification is a process that God advances in us as we meditate on Him, or, as Ephesians 4 puts it, as we: 1) grow up into Him; 2) are renewed in the spirit of

our minds (meditating on Him in the Word); and 3) are perfected through the knowledge of Him.

Rather than emphasizing what teens need to do, we need to
help them learn to meditate upon the person and character of
the Godhead in the Word. As they become competent in that
exercise, God will perfect and transform them "from glory to
glory" (2 Cor. 3:18). This is a gradual, daily, step-by-step walk.

Man-focused sanctification emphasizes my efforts, the
steps I need to take to overcome various sins, and the steps
I need to take to put on godly qualities. However, a God-focused approach to sanctification will emphasize the imperative
of learning to meditate on God in the Word. As we grow in
our knowledge of Him, God will progressively sanctify us, or
change us into the image of His Son.

Does that mean we have no responsibility to "put off"
our old way of life and "put on" the new way? The answer is
obvious. We are responsible. The question is not whether or
not we are responsible to put off sinful habits and put on the
righteousness of Christ. The question is how that is accomplished. It is *not* accomplished by developing "steps" or setting
up "methods" for change. Sanctification (including the gradual
putting off and putting on) is accomplished by God, not by us,
when we meditate upon Him in His Word.

ON HOW WE VIEW SERVICE

Finally, a God-focused mindset will change the way a believer serves the Lord. We can serve because we feel it is our
duty, or we can serve because His Word is in us as a burning
fire so that we cannot help but serve (Jer. 20:9).

Teens (and adults) are often shamed into serving. Perhaps they are told that if they don't serve, they are not right with God, or that they are desperately needed in the choir or some other place. Perhaps young people may serve because they feel it is their duty to do so. Too often this kind of service is accompanied by grumbling, by complaining that no one else is doing their fair share, and by a lack of faithfulness. Why? They are manipulated by guilt, not motivated by God's grace. The focus is on a job that needs to be done and the duty to do it. The focus is not on God!

A God-focused approach to service is different. It comes from an inner urge and zeal for God. When a person is filled with love and awe for what His God has done for him, service will be voluntary, faithfully performed, and joyfully pursued. It is like the fire burning in Jeremiah's heart. He tried to quit but couldn't. God's Word had made such an impact upon him that he could not quit. Paul described this divine power by saying that "the love of Christ" controlled him (2 Cor. 5:14).

Emphasize the person and work of God in your teaching and counseling. Help your students to grow in their knowledge of Him. Teach them how to meditate upon Him in the Word and in His works. Soon, they will look for ways to serve Him in your class. It will be a service that derives from a heart that is filled with the knowledge of God.

CHAPTER 5

WHAT MUST
I DO NEXT?

We have seen the value and the imperative of having a God-focused school and classroom. But that begs this question: How do I go about doing it? What do you need to do next? Consider the six suggestions that follow.

MAKE SURE THAT *YOU* ARE GOD-FOCUSED

A God-focused classroom begins with you—the teacher. In 1 Timothy 4:12, Paul reminds Timothy that he must set the example. If you are not God-focused, you can't expect your students to be God-focused. Being God-focused is what you do daily, not what you do once a week or for a set number of days that you determine to be God-focused. It doesn't work to say, "Hey, you know, this book is challenging. I think I'll have a God-focused emphasis in my classroom for the next couple of weeks." That's not good enough.

A God-focus must become a part of you. It must become a mindset. It must so grip your thinking process that it affects what you do every day of your life. It must become natural. It must drive you and motivate you. If you would be an instrument for heart change—a cardiologist—start with your own heart. Then, you can begin to affect the hearts of your students.

TEACH EVERY SUBJECT FROM A GOD-FOCUSED PERSPECTIVE

Whether you teach math or geography; history or English; Bible or biology, you must seek to associate it with the character and work of God. Science certainly reflects the character and wisdom of God. Math shows His orderliness, His wisdom, and His design. Geography shows His plan for the world.

Practice seeking to magnify His majesty no matter the subject. Lift Him up. Talk about who He is and how awesome He is. Your goal should be that your students will leave your class saying, "What a wonderful God I have!" Exalt Him. Magnify Him in your teaching.

MAKE MUCH OF PRAYER

Make much of prayer in your classroom. Prayer is a natural reaction to love for Almighty God. When students mention problems in their lives, lead the entire class to bow right then and to implore God to work on their behalf. Do not rush through your prayer, saying the obvious and using the same old tired cliché's and phrases. When you pray, pause. Truly talk to God. Talk to Him about your students in front of the entire class—audibly, passionately, and carefully.

We cheapen God and prayer when we glibly say a few words and then rush into the lesson. Prayer is entering the majestic throne room of God. There is a sublime reverence in entering into union with God in prayer. Show it! Let your students sense that you are serious about prayer. Help your students sense that you have entered the very presence of a Holy God.

EMPHASIZE GOD-FOCUSED SCRIPTURE MEMORY

If your Bible curriculum does not provide a Scripture memory program, develop one that deals with the person and attributes of God. Take one or two verses every week and memorize them, discussing what the attribute means, how it is seen in the verse, and what it means to the students' lives.

EMPHASIZE MEDITATION ON GOD IN THE WORD

Make much of meditation on God in the Word. Show them how. Take a sheet of paper and let them draw a line down the middle to about one-third of the way to the bottom. Then draw a line across the bottom third so that you have divided your paper into three sections. In the top left section have them write: "What God did." In the top right section have them write: "Who God is" (His attributes). In the bottom section, which stretches across the page, have them write: "How God works." *(See the sample illustration on the next page.)*

Next, assign a passage for them to read, and let them fill out the three sections as they read—focusing totally on what God did, who God is, and how God works. Give them a few minutes to complete the form, and then allow time to discuss what they saw.

After several days of practicing this discipline, their skills will improve, and they will begin to understand the value of focusing on God in the Word. For other ideas on God-focused devotions, check out the *Top Priority: Manna* series available at the Positive Action web site.

What God did:	Who God is:
How God works:	

PROVIDE OPPORTUNITIES FOR "WORKS OF GOD" TESTIMONIES

Students at a Bible college in the Midwest regularly set aside a time for "Works of God" testimonies in chapel. They build a biography of God by recording things they see Him do in their lives and answers to prayer He gives.

Have your students keep a "Works of God" journal. Every time God works in your classroom or in the life of one of your students, lead the entire class to record it in their journals. Once a week take a moment or two to let different students give their testimonies of the greatness of God in their lives the past week. You can fuel the discussion by asking questions:

"Did any of you see the omniscience (omnipotence, etc.) of God this week?"

"Did anyone have a special answer to prayer this week?"

"What is the best thing you learned about your Lord this week?"

"Are there special areas in which we need to see God work this week?"

Students need opportunities to express their praise and their love for God publicly. The expressing of their praise and love will only deepen their God-focus.

CONCLUSION

One final word of caution must be noted. One of the most dangerous things a teacher can do is to conform behavior but fail to deal with the heart. Such behavior is *always* temporary because the body is ultimately controlled by the heart. And as soon as the outward pressure of parents, youth group, school, or church is removed, the body will follow the heart. Give your students a heart for God. Obedience, not merely behavior, will follow. The heart of the matter is a matter of the heart.